REA·SONS
MY KID IS
CRY·ING

GREG PEMBROKE

REA·SONS
MY KID IS
CRY·ING

 THREE RIVERS PRESS · NEW YORK

Copyright © 2014 by Greg Pembroke

All rights reserved.
Published in the United States by Three Rivers Press, an imprint of the Crown Publishing Group, a division of Random House LLC, a Penguin Random House Company, New York.
www.crownpublishing.com

Three Rivers Press and the Tugboat design are registered trademarks of Random House LLC.

Library of Congress Cataloging-in-Publication Data is available upon request.

ISBN 978-0-8041-3983-0
eBook ISBN 978-0-8041-3984-7

Printed in the United States of America

BOOK DESIGN BY ELINA D. NUDELMAN
COVER DESIGN BY JESS MORPHEW
COVER PHOTOGRAPHS: (FRONT) THE PEMBROKE FAMILY; (BACK) CLOCKWISE, STARTING FROM TOP LEFT: BLAKE; J.S.K.; KATE HALVORSON; MELVIN, CAREY, AND CADEN LITTON; JESSICA METZGER AND INGRID; THE PEMBROKE FAMILY; ANDREA K.; THE CHANCE FAMILY

10 9 8 7 6 5 4 3 2 1

First Edition

TO MY FAMILY.
WE LAUGH TOGETHER. WE CRY TOGETHER.
WE MADE A BOOK TOGETHER
(WHILE LAUGHING ABOUT CRYING).

CONTENTS

INTRODUCTION *11*

PART ONE

1. Great Expectations *15*
2. Recipe for Disaster *33*
3. No Shirt, No Shoes, No Tantrum *53*
4. E.T. . . . The Exasperated Toddler *69*
5. If You Can't Do the Time *81*
6. Lost in Translation *95*
7. Pull-ups and Let-downs *107*

PART TWO

8. We Are Family   *123*

9. Sibling Rivalry   *137*

PART THREE

10. Call of the Wild   *153*

11. Higher Learning   *169*

12. It's My Party   *185*

ACKNOWLEDGMENTS   *197*

PHOTO CREDITS   *199*

REA·SONS MY KID IS CRY·ING

INTRODUCTION

When I decided to change jobs and stay at home two days per week with two sons under two years old, I knew things would get crazy, but no one could have predicted how crazy they would get. Kids cry for any and all reasons—and despite how hard you try to prevent the meltdowns, they still crash down on your head like so many waves of tortured sadness. Desperate to find a laugh in this sea of tears, I started snapping pictures midtantrum. Nearly two years into this experiment in Daddy Daycare, my Tumblr blog *Reasons My Son Is Crying* was born. Part documentary, part therapy, and completely hilarious, submissions immediately began pouring in from parents around the world. This collection of photos—from both my house and families across six continents—is a glimpse into the tribulations of parenthood and a sweet reminder to find a way to laugh at these tumultuous, tedious, and terrible twos. And threes. And fours. Maybe fives.

PART ONE

1
GREAT EXPECTATIONS

Like tiny Bond villains with very small and insanely specific goals, toddlers have great expectations for what life will bring on any given day. Disappoint them at your peril.

DISPATCHES · FROM · THE · FRONT · LINES

The great thing about kids is that because they know so little of the world, everything is new and exciting to them. Recently my son and I were having a great time wrestling on the floor, laughing and giggling—a perfect father-son moment.

That is, until he started staring at my hands. I guess he had never noticed my knuckles before. He hated the look of that weird, wrinkly, bunched-up skin—and started tugging on it, demanding that I "take it off." When I explained that it just wasn't possible for me to rip off my own knuckles, our fun-filled afternoon wrestlefest turned into the eighth sobbing fit of the day.

HE GOT STUCK.

2
RECIPE FOR DISASTER

Parents know that nutritious, homemade meals are necessary to make sure that your kids grow up healthy and strong. Toddlers know that mealtime is a broccoli-filled Thunderdome where only the strongest, smartest, and fastest will survive.

HIS INSTANT OATMEAL WAS NOT, IN FACT, INSTANT.

SHE DEMANDED A NEW FORK. NOW SHE WANTS THE OLD FORK BACK.

I WOULDN'T PUT SALT ON HER APRICOTS.

HER POPSICLE WAS COLD.

I LET HIM DRINK HIS
SMOOTHIE IN THE CAR.

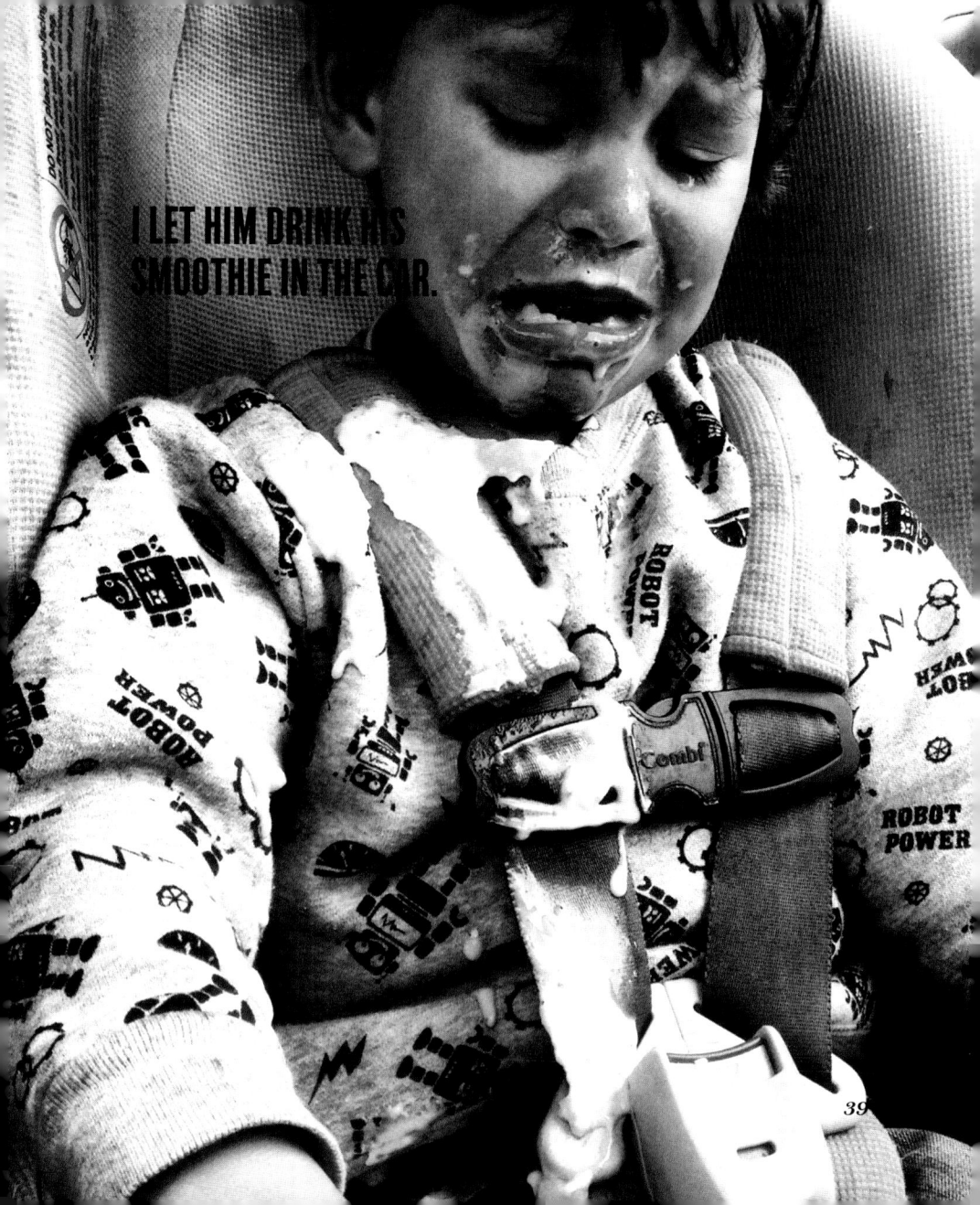

THIS TEDDY GRAHAM
LOST ITS HEAD.

WE THOUGHT HE MIGHT LIKE TO TRY PEAS.

I TOOK THE GLASS OF RED WINE AWAY FROM HER.

WE HAD TO PUT THE CUPCAKES INTO THE OVEN TO BAKE.

THE LAST PIECE OF BANANA
FELL OUT OF THE PEEL.

THE BANANA IS OVER.

HE WANTED ME TO PUT THE CRUST BACK ONTO THE TOAST.

I TOLD HER THAT I HAD TO WASH HER FACE AFTER DINNER.

A FLY LANDED NEAR HIM.

I TOLD HIM TO STOP STUFFING HIS SUPPER DOWN HIS PANTS.

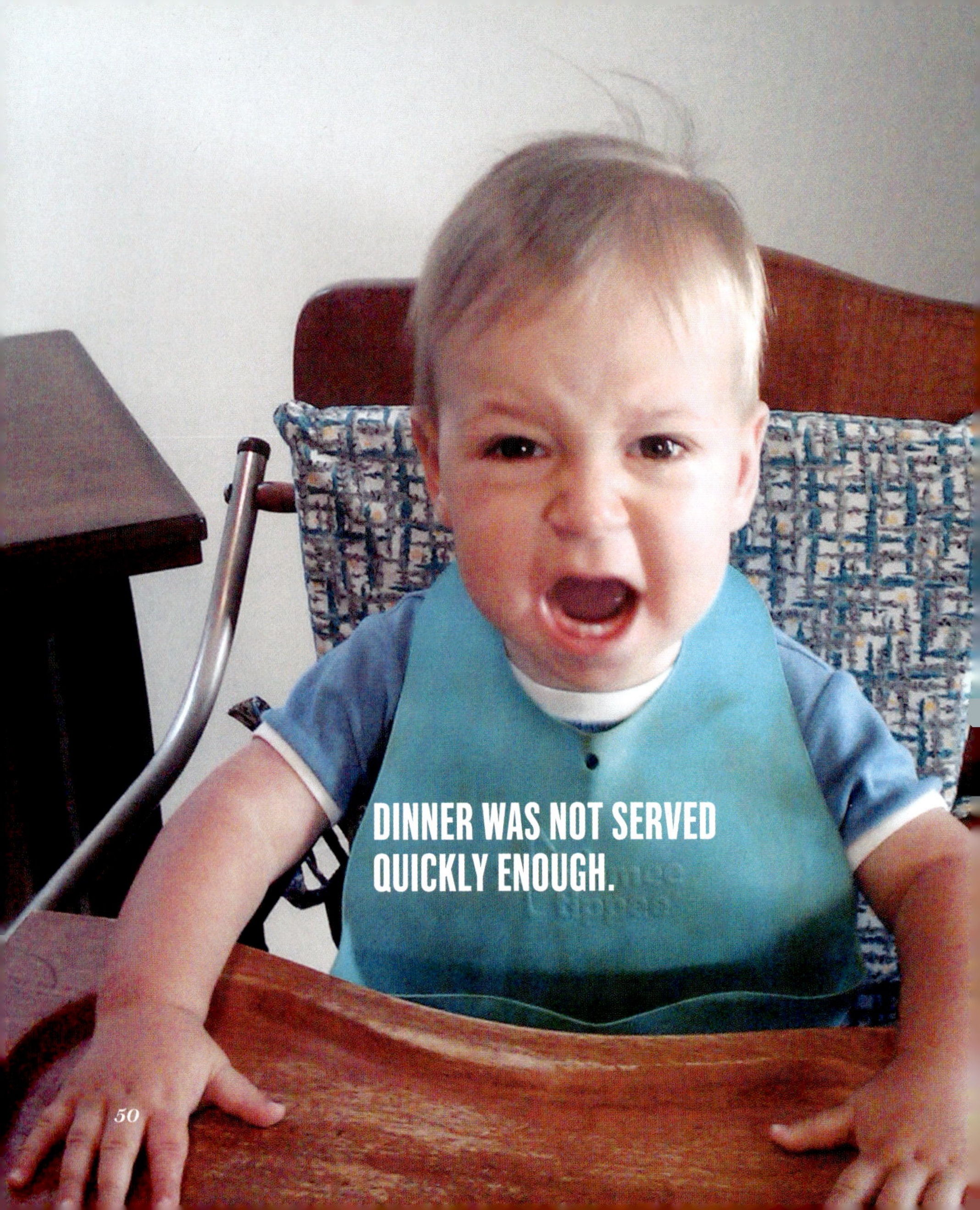

DINNER WAS NOT SERVED
QUICKLY ENOUGH.

REASONS · WHY · I'M · CRYING

- I asked him to stop using his spoon to catapult his peas across the table, one by one, like a medieval fortress siege.

- I politely asked him to stop sitting on his brother's head.

- I wouldn't let him stick a garden hose down his brother's pants.

- He happily invited me to "feel his sleeve." I did. He immediately lost his mind and said, "NOOOOO! NOT WITH YOUR HANDS!!!"

- I secretly suggested we get ice cream by spelling the word to my wife—and was immediately busted by the three-year-old, because I-C-E sounds exactly like *ice cream*.

HE WAS TRYING TO PUT HIS UNDERWEAR ON HIS HEAD. I HELPED.

3
NO SHIRT, NO SHOES, NO TANTRUM

From the earliest of ages, toddlers develop a fashion sense all their own. They have very strong opinions when it comes to their preferred wardrobe—and comfort is king. Why wear jeans when you can wear "soft pants"—or better yet, NOTHING AT ALL! From their shouts of *I can do it myself* while hopelessly lost inside their turtlenecks to their endless battles against shirt tags of all types, clothing your toddler is such a struggle that you find yourself seriously considering moving to a warmer climate.

SHE TOOK OFF HER SANDAL, THEN COULDN'T PUT IT BACK ON.

I WOULDN'T LET HIM GO OUTSIDE IN DADDY'S SHOES.

HE DIDN'T LIKE THIS
MONKEY OUTFIT.

SHE DIDN'T WANT TO BE A SAILOR LIKE HER SISTER.

HE TOOK OFF HIS SHOES AND SOCKS. HIS FEET ARE NOW COLD.

HE WANTED TO WEAR SOCKS AND FLIP-FLOPS

I TOLD HIM HE DIDN'T NEED THAT BAND-AID ANYMORE.

I TOOK OFF HIS WINTER COAT WHEN HE GOT HOME.

HE DIDN'T LIKE ANY OF THE FORTY-SIX PAIRS OF SWIMSUITS I OFFERED HIM.

DISPATCHES · FROM · THE · FRONT · LINES

One of my wife's biggest complaints about having boys is that there just aren't as many "cute" clothes for them as there are for girls. But she perseveres, scouring stores in search of outfits that will make our boys look like the most handsome prep-school gentlemen you've ever seen.

Those outfits are pristine, unworn, and hanging in the closet.

And in their place? Pajamas. At all times. We secretly hope that, when our boys grow up and perhaps get married, they'll be wearing beautifully cut suits, dazzlingly shined shoes, and elegant ties. But the smart money is on Buzz Lightyear pajamas with rocket wings.

I RECENTLY TOOK UP KNITTING AS A HOBBY.

WE HAD HIM TRY ON HIS NEW SWEATER.

HE WANTS TO
WEAR HIS BROWN
SHOES.

HE WANTS HIM TO WEAR HIS YELLOW SHOES.

HIS TRAIN DERAILED.

4
E.T. . . .
THE EXASPERATED TODDLER

As newly arrived visitors to our world, children are seeing everything on our planet for the first time. Our advanced technologies confuse and enrage them. Zippers are their vicious metal-toothed foes. Light switches are tauntingly placed far above their reach, and universal remotes are covered with hieroglyphs that must somehow be decoded before Elmo will appear. Yes, the world can be a confusing place for all of us—but especially so for a two-year-old who thinks Newton's Third Law has something to do with figs.

THE DIAPER IS GONE.

BUZZ LIGHTYEAR'S KNEE IS BENT.

**THE MODEM
STOPPED FLASHING.**

I WOULDN'T LET HIM ELECTROCUTE HIMSELF.

THE SLIDE IS NOT SLIPPERY ENOUGH.

THE DOG WAS IN THE WAY WHILE HE WAS TRYING TO PUSH THE CHAIR.

75

T-REX'S JAW IS NOT BIG ENOUGH TO BITE THIS LEGO-MAN'S HEAD.

THE REMOTE-CONTROLLED CAR HE WAS DRIVING DROVE AWAY.

REASONS · WHY · *I'M* · CRYING

- We saw a dragonfly. My son reacted like he was being attacked by a pterodactyl.

- Why do those we love most try so hard to gouge out our eyes with Matchbox cars?

- Despite my repeated pleadings, he has successfully hidden his water cup from himself again. Does that make him the winner or the loser of this game?

- My three-year-old is super, super helpful . . . as long as the task at hand is opening all his brother's birthday presents—and not sharing them.

- He gave his Slinky Dog toy to his little brother. His brother happily accepted. CUT TO SOUL-CRUSHING REALIZATION THAT HE NOW HAS NO SLINKY DOG TOY.

HER DAD IS STUCK IN THE COMPUTER.

HE PUT HIMSELF
IN TIME OUT FOR
NO REASON

5
IF YOU CAN'T DO THE TIME

Toddlers are forever pushing their boundaries—and your buttons—to see just how much they can get away with. Transitioning from caregiver to crime stopper is all part of the job. You make up the rules as you go and you try your best to enforce them, but the minute your back is turned . . .

IT WAS TIME TO TAKE A NAP.

WE TOLD HIM THE BATHTUB WAS NOT A BED.

WE EXPLAINED THAT SHE HAD TO PUT ON HER SWIMSUIT TO GO INTO THE POOL.

I TOLD HIM THE TOILET IS NOT A TOY.

HE PITCHED HIS TOYS DOWN THE STAIRS FOR THE THOUSANDTH TIME AND I SAID HE HAD TO GET THEM HIMSELF.

HE THREW HIS DINNER ON THE FLOOR AND NOW HE WANTS TO EAT.

HE WASN'T ALLOWED TO FINISH EATING THE DIAPER CREAM.

I WOULDN'T LET HIM DRIVE HIS COZY COUPE DOWN THE BASEMENT STAIRS.

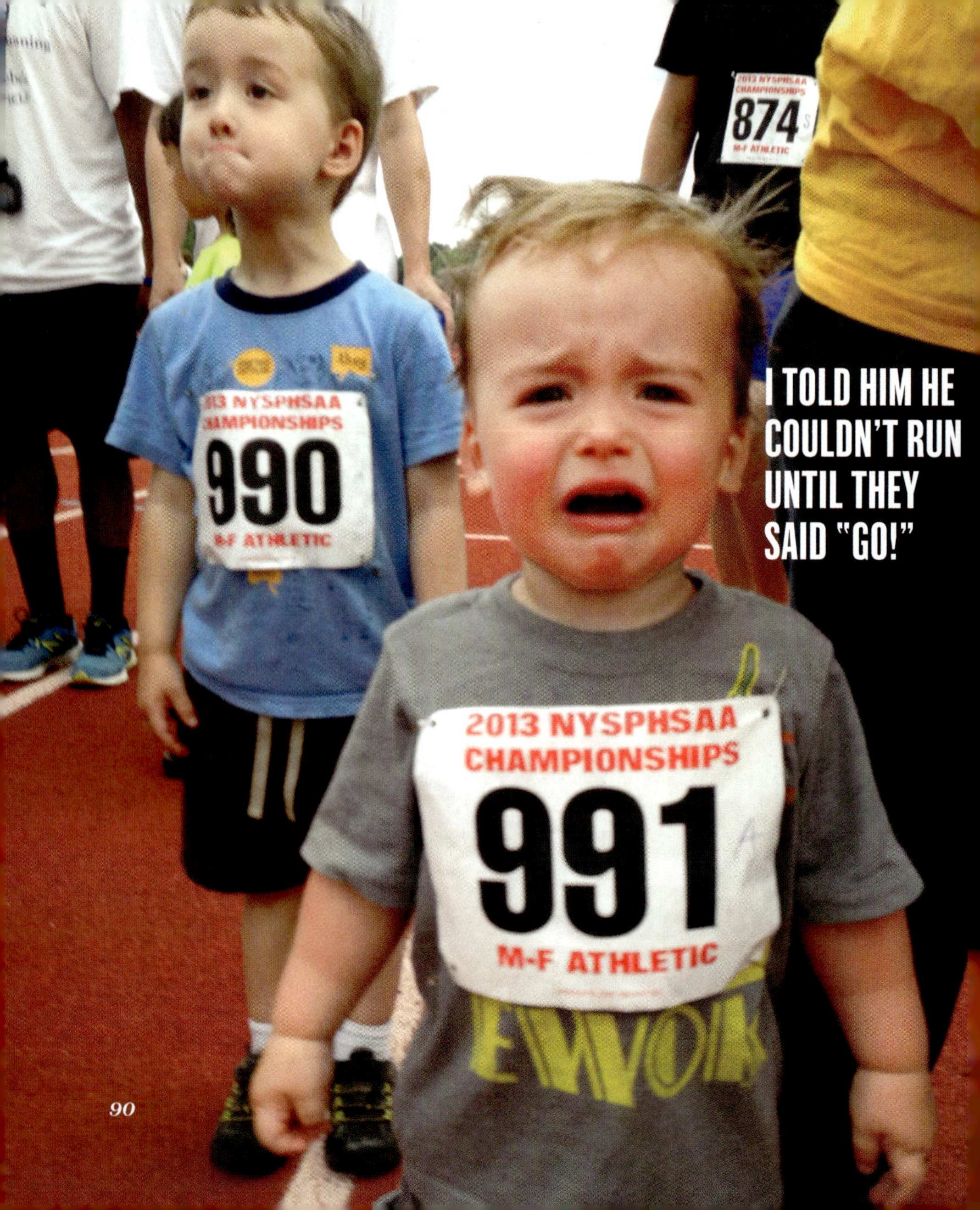

I TOLD HIM HE COULDN'T RUN UNTIL THEY SAID "GO!"

SHE'S NOT ALLOWED TO EAT GARBAGE OUT OF THE GARBAGE CAN.

REASONS · WHY · *I'M* · CRYING

- My two-year-old boy opened the door while I was on the toilet. Then my wife and three-year-old came in and we watched as he opened his birthday presents. This is not how I imagined my life would be.

- An eventful day: my two-year-old took a toy screwdriver from the toolbox, walked behind me, yelled "Get him!" and started shivving me in the neck, like in a prison riot.

- Honest admission: My dinner tonight consisted of 100 percent leftovers from my boys' plates. And beer.

- At the last second, I stopped him from drinking the cup of milk that he had successfully hidden in his toy box for at least two days.

- I suggested that maybe the ketchup was best left on the plate—not spread evenly across the table, the chairs, his face, and his brother.

WE STOPPED HIM FROM EATING THIS ROLL OF TOILET PAPER.

I ASKED HIM FOR A HIGH FIVE.

6
LOST IN TRANSLATION

One of the joys of parenthood is the passing of wisdom between the generations, the gentle flow of conversation between parent and child. Unfortunately there's no Rosetta Stone software for "toddlerese," so miscommunication seems inevitable....

WE TOLD HIM THAT HE LOOKED VERY HANDSOME.

I SAID WE HAD TO CLEAN THE CAKE OFF HER.

DISPATCHES • FROM • THE • FRONT • LINES

Recently, I tried to teach my three-year-old a joke while we were driving:

"Why did the chicken cross the road?"

"I didn't see any chickens."

"No, I didn't either, but just SAY there was a chicken who was crossing the road...."

"[Concerned] We would hit him with our car!"

"No, okay, what if there was a chicken who wanted to cross the road and there were no cars coming."

"He would FLY. Can chickens fly, Daddy?"

"Well, no. Hmmm. Maybe, for short distances? I'm actually not sure—"

"LOOK DAD . . . A HORSIE!"

It's a work in progress.

ANOTHER KID WANTED TO KNOW WHAT TOY HE WAS HOLDING—AND I TOLD HIM.

I ASKED HIM WHAT HE WANTED FOR DINNER.

I OFFERED HIM HIS FAVORITE SMOOTHIE.

I OFFERED HIM THE PHONE SO HE COULD SAY HI TO MOMMY.

I PRETENDED
MY HAND WAS A
PHONE.

HIS TEACHER SAID "NO" . . . TO SOMEONE ELSE.

SHE BIT MY FINGER.
I SAID "OUCH."

I REFUSED TO PUT MY OWN HAIR IN A PONYTAIL.

7
PULL-UPS AND LET-DOWNS

Kids know exactly how they want their world to work. They have a precise course of action—a battle plan they follow to the letter as their day unfolds. Tragically, they're utterly unable or unwilling to explain this game plan to their parents. Even the smallest of deviations from their top-secret to-do list is unacceptable. One wrong move, and you'll unwittingly unleash some of the most unexpected, unpredictable, and unreasonable face-down-on-the-ground flare-ups you have ever seen.

I GAVE HIM PEANUT BUTTER ON A SPOON INSTEAD OF ON MY FINGER.

I LEFT HER HOME WHILE I WENT TO THE STORE TO BUY CUPCAKES.

I WENT TO THE BATHROOM WITHOUT HER.

DADDY DIDN'T WANT A BATHROOM AUDIENCE.

WE ASKED HIM IF HE
WAS READY TO GO GET
ICE CREAM.

HE DIDN'T WANT TO HOLD MY HAND WHILE WALKING HOME FROM DAY CARE.

WE SIGNED HIS CAST.

I WOULDN'T RIDE WITH HER (I AM 6'4"; IT'S NOT PHYSICALLY POSSIBLE).

WE THREW HIM A PARTY AND INVITED ALL OUR FAMILY AND FRIENDS.

WE TURNED ON HIS FAVORITE SHOW THE MINUTE HE ASKED US TO.

I WENT TO THE MAILBOX, LOCATED ONE FOOT AWAY FROM THE FRONT DOOR.

WE TOLD HIM WE COULDN'T AFFORD A COLOR TELEVISION.

Retro Tantrum

PART TWO

HIS AUNT WOULDN'T LET HIM PLAY WITH THIS AX.

122

8
WE ARE FAMILY

Nothing brings a family together like the introduction of a new baby. The minute that precious bundle of joy arrives home from the hospital, swarms of aunts, uncles, and grandparents arrive—eager to shower these little angels with their love and affection. This doesn't always go as planned.

HE WANTED HIS PICTURE TAKEN, BUT NOT WITH DADDY.

SHE DIDN'T WANT TO SHARE THE POOL WITH NANA.

HIS UNCLE GAVE HIM A HUG.

DADDY THOUGHT IT WOULD BE FUN TO TAKE HIM TO A POOL.

I LET GO OF HIS HAND TO SHOW HIS GRANDMA HOW WELL HE COULD WALK.

WE TOLD HER SHE HAD TO TAKE OFF GRANDMA'S GLASSES SO THAT SHE COULD SEE.

HE COULDN'T CARRY THE BREAKFAST UP TO DADDY ON FATHER'S DAY.

HIS SKYPE CHAT WITH GRANDMA AND GRANDPA FROZE.

SHE DIDN'T RECOGNIZE DADDY IN HIS CONTACTS.

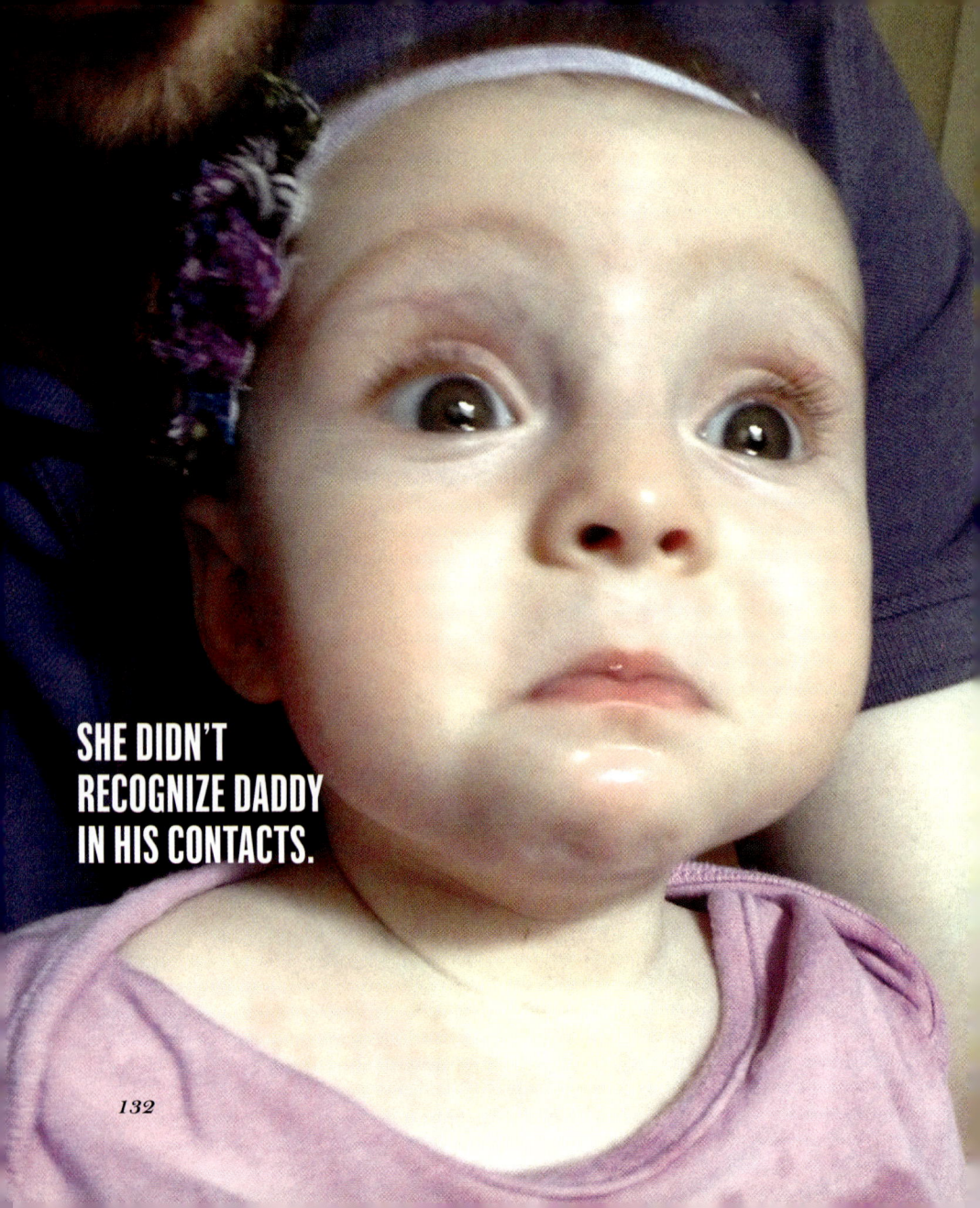

GRANDMA WOULDN'T LET HIM SPILL HIS ICE WATER ALL OVER THE TABLE (AND HER LAP).

REASONS · WHY · *I'M* · CRYING

- It's 85 degrees and he wanted to wear long-sleeved fleece pj's and a blanket. I said that he might be hot. He vehemently disagreed.

- We arrived at our fifth toddler birthday party in the past two weeks . . . and realized that we had left the gift on the roof of the car. Classic.

- I suggested that maybe we shouldn't put our books, toys, and toothbrushes on top of the toilet. I know! Crazy talk.

- I wouldn't let him take off his diaper and "go commando" while jumping on my bed, directly over my head.

- Sometimes, I stay up wondering what I'm going to step on next in my bare feet. I bet either a grape or a dinosaur. Hopefully not a triceratops.

SHE IS A FLOWER GIRL AT HER COUSIN'S WEDDING.

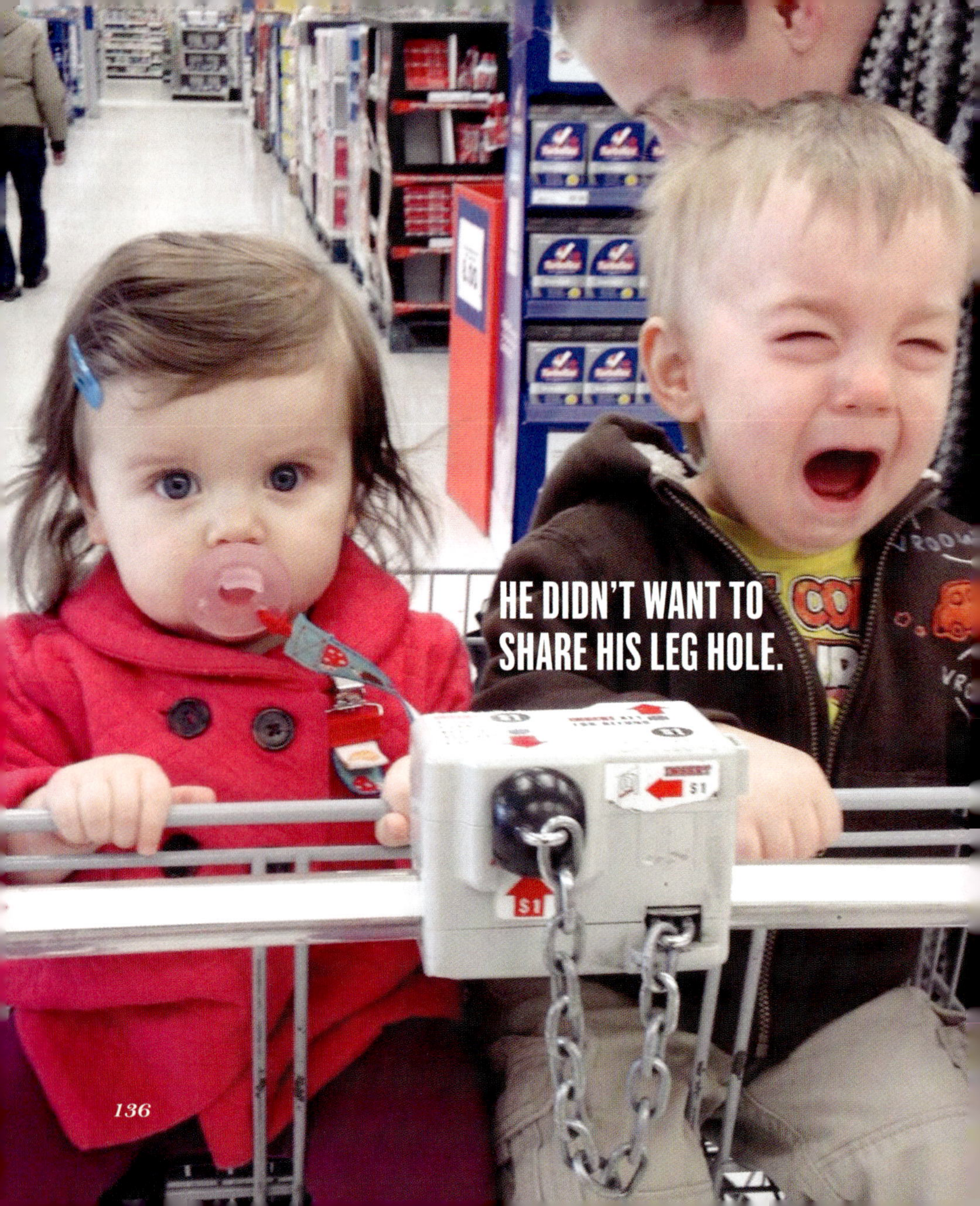

HE DIDN'T WANT TO SHARE HIS LEG HOLE.

9
SIBLING RIVALRY

Siblings are the best friends we never asked for. It's no wonder that the source of the greatest joy and pain in the lives of toddlers comes from the people on the planet who they are genetically closest to.

WE TOLD HER THAT SHE WAS GOING TO HAVE A BABY BROTHER.

HE WOULDN'T SHARE HIS WATER.

I THOUGHT WE COULD TAKE A CUTE "BIG BROTHER–LITTLE BROTHER" PICTURE.

DISPATCHES • FROM • THE • FRONT • LINES

Like most parents, we have extolled the healing virtues of kisses for all manner of injuries over the years, from bumped heads to scraped knees. The other day, I heard my older boy crying. I ran into the bedroom to see his little brother hitting him in the head, and then immediately kissing it to make it "all better" ... and then hitting him again. After turning my head so they couldn't see me laughing, I tried my best to explain that it didn't work quite like that....

HIS BROTHER DOESN'T UNDERSTAND WHAT "PERSONAL SPACE" MEANS.

HER BROTHER SAT DOWN.

HIS SISTER BLOCKED HIS KICK.

HER SISTER CAUGHT A FISH.

I TOLD THEM THAT I LOVED THEM BOTH EQUALLY.

THEY GOT CAUGHT BETWEEN THE SPEAKER AND THE COUCH.

HER SISTER GAVE HER A KISS.

HER BROTHER SAID
SHE COULD GO FIRST.
FOR A SHOT.

PART THREE

HE DOESN'T LIKE THE GRASS.

10
CALL OF THE WILD

Almost as important as sleep and good nutrition, time spent outdoors is a critical component of toddler happiness. Like the Lewis and Clark of suburbia, children set forth to explore the world—unfortunately stopping to inspect every pebble, flower, beetle, and ant (and goose dropping) along the way.

WATER GOT ON HIS BATHING SUIT.

SHE HAS TO WEAR A HAT WHILE OUTSIDE.

I WOULDN'T LET HIM PLAY WITH THE DEAD SQUIRREL HE FOUND IN THE YARD.

I TOOK THE ROCKS SHE WAS CHEWING OUT OF HER MOUTH.

I TOLD HIM THAT HE COULDN'T GO TO THE BATHROOM ON OUR NEIGHBOR'S LAWN.

WE LET HIM PLAY OUTSIDE IN THE RAIN.

THE SAND MADE HIS FEET SANDY.

THE WIND WASN'T WINDY.

SHE WAS SPLASHED.

HE RAN OUT OF TOYS TO
THROW INTO HIS POOL.

DISPATCHES • FROM • THE • FRONT • LINES

A typical trip to the playground for our energetic explorers can include any one of the following time-honored toddler activities:

1. Crying because I made them go to the playground
2. Crying because no other children are there
3. Crying because too many other children are there
4. Crying because the laws of physics won't allow the swing to go any higher
5. Crying because I won't let them chew old gum found on a bench
6. Crying because I won't let them throw sand
7. Crying because they had sand thrown at them
8. Crying because I won't let them fall from high places
9. Crying because it's time to go home

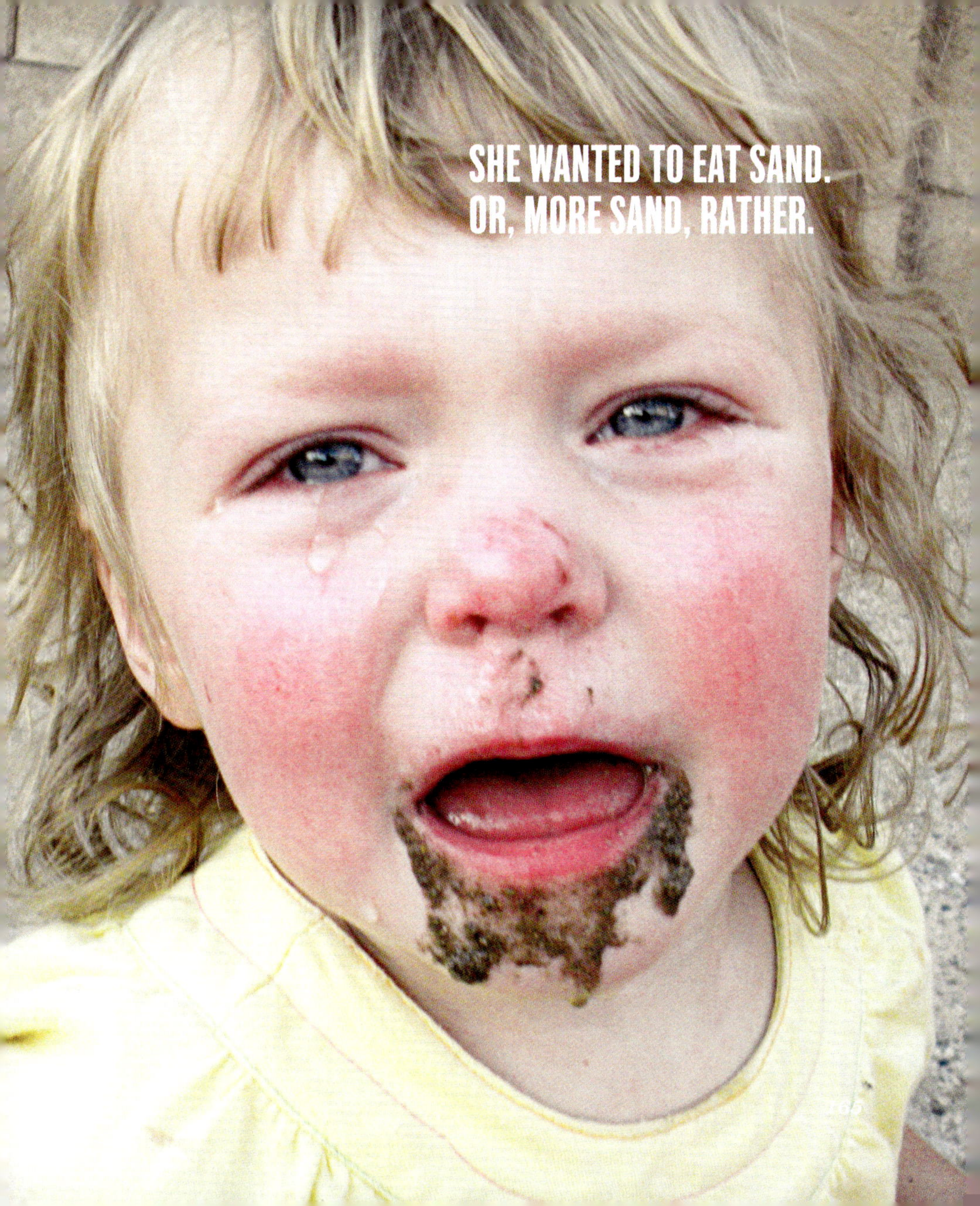
SHE WANTED TO EAT SAND.
OR, MORE SAND, RATHER.

I PUT HER ON A WOBBLY LOG.

HE COULDN'T WALK THROUGH THE PLAYGROUND'S SAFETY SCREEN.

167

THE OFFICERS LET HIM SIT ON THIS MOTORCYCLE.

11
HIGHER LEARNING

A key element of safeguarding and shepherding your young charges through the world is to present them with a wide array of age-appropriate and endlessly stimulating educational experiences that they will remember forever. Broadening horizons and leaving an indelible intellectual mark, these unforgettable days form the men and women of tomorrow.

THE AQUARIUM DOESN'T OPEN FOR TEN MORE MINUTES.

HE COULDN'T PLAY IN OLD FAITHFUL AT YELLOWSTONE NATIONAL PARK.

WE WOULDN'T LET HIM THROW HIS DAD'S GLASSES DOWN INTO THIS LIGHTHOUSE.

I TOLD HIM THAT WE WERE GOING TO THE ZOO.

WE TOOK HIM TO A PETTING ZOO.

WE COULDN'T TAKE THE
LIONS HOME WITH US.

DISPATCHES · FROM · THE · FRONT · LINES

We thought for sure that a visit to "Sue," the most complete T-Rex fossil skeleton ever assembled, would be the perfect thing for our dino-loving boys. And it was! Imagine our joy and satisfaction as the boys stared in amazement at this truly larger-than-life creature looming over us.

Then imagine our horror as they attempted to run under the velvet ropes and grab hold of her almost-70-million-year-old legs! As a wise man once said, you can lead a horse to water, but you can't keep a toddler from trying to destroy priceless tyrannosaurus bones.

I WOULDN'T LET HIM EAT THIS UNSWEETENED COCOA POWDER BY THE SPOONFUL.

I SAID I WOULDN'T GIVE HIM ANY MORE BOOKS.

WE BOUGHT HIM SOME EDIBLE FINGER PAINTS.

THE GOAT GOT A LITTLE TOO CLOSE.

180

THE FARM ANIMALS WERE TOO LOUD.

HE DIDN'T WANT TO RIDE ON A TRAIN.

HE MET BILL MURRAY.

183

WE TOOK HER TO SEE SANTA.

12
IT'S MY PARTY

Birthdays, holidays, and special occasions. It's your time to make those magical memories that will last a lifetime. These are the highlights of the toddler calendar, and all your family and friends are invited. Welcome to the Super Bowl of parenting.

WE THOUGHT A PHOTO WITH THE EASTER BUNNY WOULD MAKE HIM EXCITED FOR OUR EGG HUNT.

WE GAVE HIM HIS OWN "BUNNY EARS" FOR EASTER.

WE ASKED HIM TO TRY ON HIS COSTUME, JUST TO MAKE SURE IT FIT.

SHE DOESN'T WANT TO BE THE PINK UNICORN.

HE ASKED WHAT TOYS HE WANTED FOR CHRISTMAS.

SANTA BOUGHT HIM A NEW BALANCE BIKE.

THERE WERE NO MORE PRESENTS TO OPEN.

DISPATCHES · FROM · THE · FRONT · LINES

Holidays are a time when families get together to celebrate togetherness and giving.

Our older boy had a fire truck toy that he loves. Unfortunately, our younger boy soon started to love it as well. The fur began to fly and fights over the fire truck were a daily occurrence, so we decided that a new, identical truck would make the perfect Christmas gift for our two-year-old.

After several weeks of looking, we finally found one for sale, wrapped it up, then waited for the joyful day. Upon opening it, my sons realized that it was indeed identical—except for one single sticker that was torn. Instead of happily playing alongside each other with their identical trucks, the boys then fought over which one would get the one with the torn sticker.

Like I said, holidays are a time when families . . .

WE WOULDN'T LET HIM TOUCH THE FIRE.

WE GATHERED AROUND AND YELLED "HAPPY BIRTHDAY!"

I HAVE NO IDEA WHY MY SON IS CRYING.

ACKNOWLEDGMENTS

I would like to offer my sincerest thanks to the thousands of families who submitted photos for this book and for my website. It's a truly remarkable community that we have established—and I can't wait to see what hilarious photos you'll send me next!

To Charity: Knowing you'll be there for me, for better or worse, is the reason we have so much "for better" and so little "for worse." I promise to someday not spend so much time on my phone.

And of course I would be utterly remiss not to also thank my beautiful crying boys. I know we choose to celebrate some of the silly reasons for your tears, but always remember that the laughter and joy you both bring washes away any sadness, tenfold. The last four and a half years have been an incredible journey, and I cannot wait to relish the adventures, hilarity, and mischief that await us all as a family in the future!

PHOTO CREDITS

Page 14: Kate Halvorson; page 16: Amy; page 17: Jamie; page 18: Benji; page 19: Elissa Kojzarek; page 20: David Barendt and Robin Jump; page 21: The Baker Family; page 22: Rebecca Stachewicz; page 23: Lara Dolly Elliman; page 24: Emily Hannux; page 25: The Sitko Family; page 27: Rebecca Stachewicz; page 28: The Chance Family; page 29: The Gould Family; page 30: The Pembroke Family; page 31: Rachel Lutz; page 32: Alicia Hupageman; page 34: Angie Palmer and Rachel Zabala; page 35: Bethany Beams; page 36: Chloe Wright; page 37: J. Perry; page 38: Sarah R.; page 39: Heidi Ring; page 40: Luke Shinners; page 41: Georgie Kester; page 42: Jessica Metzger and Ingrid; page 43: Ruthann Richardson and Ron Young; page 44: Rebecca S.; page 45: Sidney F.; page 46: Nate Hofer; page 47: The Yee Family; page 48: Melvin, Carey, and Caden Litton; page 49: Kyle and Jamie Anderson; page 50: Finn Jackson; page 52: Stenger Family; page 54: Chloe Wright; page 55: Heather A.; page 56: The Pembroke Family; page 57: The Yaeger Family; page 58: The Pembroke Family; page 59: Beth Mattson; page 60: The Pembroke Family; page 61: Paolo K.; page 62: Myrick Kestenbaum; page 64: The Wallevand Family; page 65: Jesse and Matt Bell (and Andy); page 66: The Pembroke Family; page 67: The Pembroke Family; page 68: The Miller Family; page 70:

Milo; page 71: The Pembroke Family; page 72: Sweet Isla Popageer; page 73: Landon Bixman; page 74: The Pembroke Family; page 75: Leif Christensen and Hunter; page 76: Quentin Jones; page 77: The Natour Family; page 79: Laurie, Joseph, and Adelyn; page 80: Kim Hendricks; page 82: Ben and Kelly Weber; page 83: The Miller Family; page 84: Nicole Aradas; page 85: B. Carothers; page 86: The Pembroke Family; page 87: The Pembroke Family; page 88: The Heskett Family; page 89: Kathy Schwerdt; page 90: The Pembroke Family; page 91: Cheryl Ruyle; page 93: The Rhoads Family; page 94: Jacob Cohen; page 96: Calvin Pence; page 97: Mike, Katie, and Aubrey; page 99: The Frisby Family; page 100: Blake; page 101: The Duzhnikovs of Dubai; page 102: The Watson Family; page 103: Jennifer Avenel; page 104: Anonymous; page 105: Ella Avery and the Capron Family; page 106: Julianne Healey; page 108: Katee and Derrick Sullivan; page 109: Sarah R.; page 110: Anonymous; page 111: The Childs Family; page 112: Jossef Dantas; page 113: Jessica Ainley-Smith; page 114: Kelly Jones; page 115: Grace Stahlman; page 116: Jesse and Matt Bell (and Andy); page 117: Nathan and Rosey Sumrall; page 118: Gayle Kesten; page 119: Sidney Kirschner; page 122: Abbey Moore and Aiden Ferrell; page 124: Kristina Campbell; page 125: Michele Hughes and Madeline Cifuni; page 126: Itay Azriel; page 127: Jillian, James, and Owen Dailey; page 128: The Heskett Family; page 129: cassady jane lorentzen; page 130: Jackson Ramey; page 131: S., S., and Z. White; page 132: The Moskowitz Family; page 133: The Pembroke Family;

page 135: Kate R.; page 136: Cheryl and Martha; page 138: Andrea Bible; page 139: Casper and Abbot; page 140: Megan Barnstable; page 142: The Pembroke Family; page 143: Jennifer Avenel; page 144: Luciano M.; page 145: Heather M.; page 146: The Pembroke Family; page 147: Carlos and Jenny Yepez; page 148: Shannon and Katelyn Ferran; page 149: The Gould Family; page 152: Nicole Aradas; page 154: Zachy; page 155: The Pepe Family; page 156: Amy and Lucas Delmanto; page 157: The Plude Family; page 158: Twist Photography; page 159: Paula and Ethan Brown; page 160: Nathaniel Anderson Patten (by Tina Yee-Patten); page 161: T.J. Hannigan; page 162: Lila Taylor; page 163: Dave Gouveia; page 165: Shilo; page 166: Beatrice Foster; page 167: Wrigley Muldoon; page 168: Lorenzo Yim (Proud of you guys); page 170: Claire; page 171: Molly O'Connor; page 172: Samuel Lamarre and Christine Labrie; page 173: The Hamilton Family; page 174: Jacob S.; page 175: The Hill Family; page 177: The Pembroke Family; page 178: Sarah K. Burkhalter; page 179: The Forr Family; page 180: The Sutton Family; page 181: The Walsh Family; page 182: Andras Szocs and Kathy Kondor; page 183: Laura, Alexander (and Bill); page 184: Jeanne Taylor Photography; page 186: Anonymous; page 187: Jesse and Matt Bell (and Andy); page 188: J.S.K.; page 189: The Oettinger Family; page 190: Andrea K.; page 191: The Thompson Family; page 192: Jennifer Avenel; page 194: Lydia S. and James S.; page 195: Ella Avery and the Capron Family; page 196: The Pembroke Family; pages 202–208: YOU!

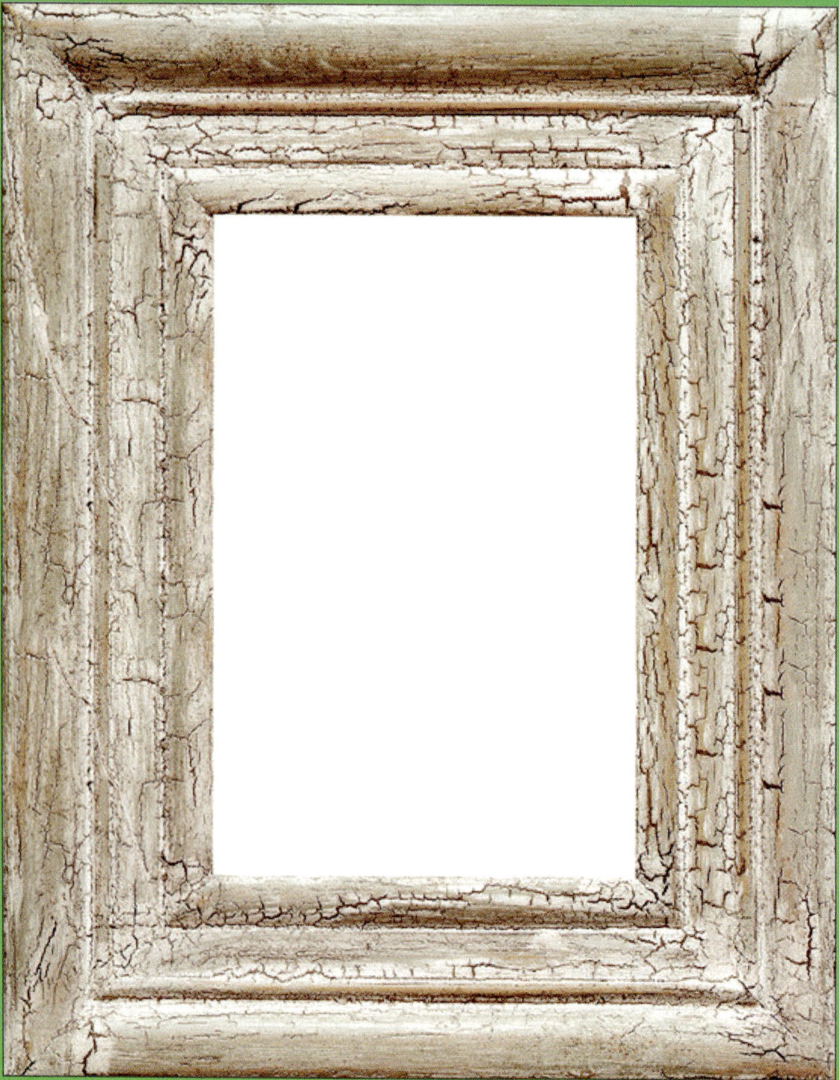

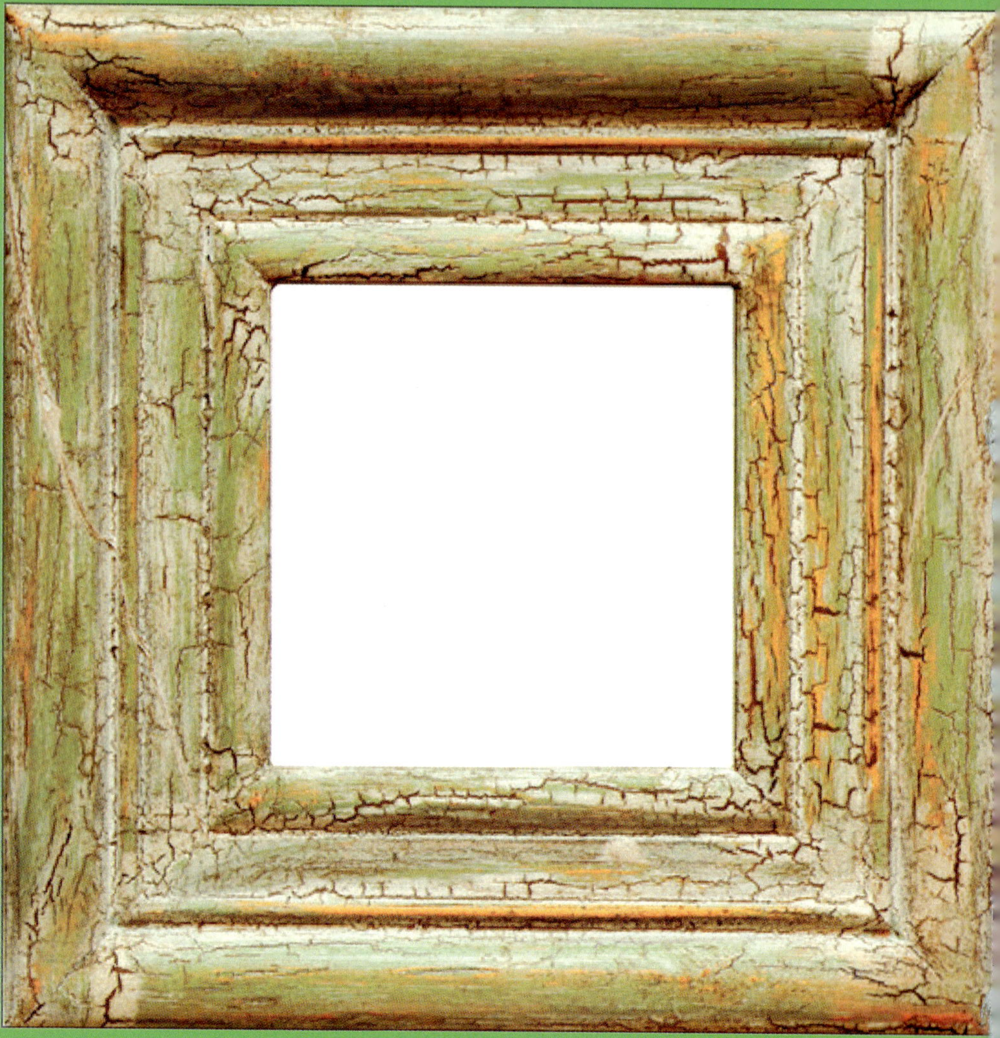